Story Sparks for Teens - 180 Visual Story Starters to Write in 10 Minutes a Day

A semester length companion designed for classrooms, after school clubs, and individual teens who want quick inspiration without feeling overwhelmed.

Morgan Hale

Copyright © 2025 by Morgan Hale

All rights reserved.

No part of this book may be reproduced in any form or by any electronic or mechanical means, including information storage and retrieval systems, without written permission from the author, except for the use of brief quotations in a book review.

PERMISSIONS AND USE

Educators may make minimal photocopies of individual prompt pages for one classroom or learning group. For wider distribution, district use, or digital sharing, please obtain permission from the publisher to ensure safe and legal use of the content.

Parents and writers may use prompts for personal creative practice, journaling, or creative writing groups.

For inquiries: contact Voyage & Quill via Nielsen

Contents

How to Use This Book	ix
Introduction for Teens	xi
Teacher and Parent Guide	xiii
1. Identity and Inner Worlds	1
2. Friends and Drama	13
3. Future Worlds	25
4. What If	37
5. First Times	49
6. Villains and Secrets	61
About the Author	73
NOTES FOR EDUCATORS	75
INDEX BY THEME	77

For every young writer who ever needed a spark.

Your stories matter.

Thank you to the teachers, librarians, parents, and mentors who create spaces where teens can imagine, explore, and express themselves freely. This book is inspired by your encouragement and your belief in young voices.

How to Use This Book

This book is designed for ten minutes a day. Each page gives you a visual idea, a short scene to begin your writing, and a Level Up challenge that you can choose to use or skip. Some prompts will feel easy. Some will feel strange. Let your imagination roam without worrying about perfection.

If you are using this book with a class, the structure allows for daily writing practice, theme based work, or creative warm ups. If you are writing on your own, you can follow the book in order or pick a page that suits your mood.

There is no wrong way to use these prompts. What matters is showing up for ten minutes and letting the ideas flow.

Introduction for Teens

Welcome to *Story Sparks for Teens*. This book gives you small creative moments that fit into real life. You do not need long stories or big ideas. You only need time, curiosity, and a willingness to try.

Each page begins with a visual spark that hints at a moment or emotion. Look at it and see what it brings up. Then read the story starter and begin writing. Some days you will write fast. Some days slowly. Both count.

The Level Up box offers an optional challenge. Try it when you want something extra. Ignore it when you just want a simple warm up.

By the end of these one hundred eighty prompts, you will have created a collection of stories, ideas, and characters that belong only to you. Your voice will grow stronger each day you write. Your stories are waiting.

Teacher and Parent Guide

Story Sparks for Teens supports creativity, narrative thinking, confidence building, and self expression. The prompts are arranged in six themed sections that connect to common classroom topics and developmental stages.

Daily warm up

Choose one prompt per day. Ten minutes of consistent writing improves fluency and reduces anxiety about getting started.

Choice based writing

Let students pick any prompt in the current section. Choice supports motivation.

Visual discussion

Use the artwork to spark conversation. Ask what students notice before writing.

Revision practice

Once a week, select one short piece and develop it further. This models the writing process.

Sharing moments

Encourage students to read a line or two with a partner or group. Sharing builds confidence and strengthens community.

At home

Parents can participate by asking about the prompt of the day or reading a favorite sentence. Small interactions help teens feel supported without pressure.

Chapter 1
Identity and Inner Worlds

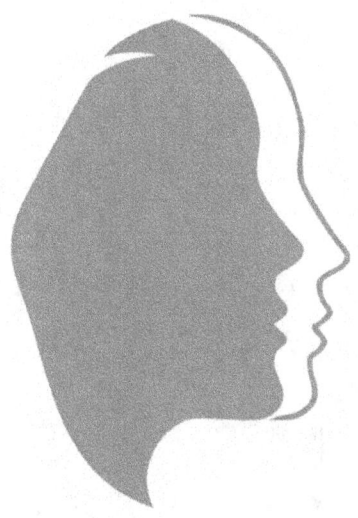

Identity is shaped by the quiet moments we often keep to ourselves. These prompts explore memory, emotion, imagination, and the inner spaces where thoughts become stories.

The visual sparks are symbolic and dreamlike.

Let them guide you into characters who are discovering who they are or who they might become.

"The Memory That Slipped Out"

1. The Reflection That Paused

Visual description: A character stands before a mirror. The room behind them is ordinary, but the reflection lags slightly behind the real movement.

Story starter: When she looked into the mirror that morning, the reflection paused for a heartbeat before matching her.

Level Up: Write a short scene from the reflection's point of view.

---

2. A Diary Entry That Was Never Meant to Be Found

Visual description: A diary lies open with a half written page. The handwriting is rushed and uneven.

Story starter: The diary entry ended in the middle of a sentence. It felt like someone had been interrupted.

Level Up: Reveal who finds the diary and why they decided to read it.

---

3. The Memory That Slipped Out

Visual description: A glass jar with glowing fragments drifting upward like tiny floating scenes.

Story starter: One memory escaped and hovered in the air. He reached for it without knowing what he was about to remember.

Level Up: Write the scene as if the memory is alive.

4. Voices in the Quiet Room

Visual description: Sunlight streams into an empty room. Soft outlines of speech bubbles drift near the walls.

Story starter: The room was silent, yet someone seemed to be whispering from a corner she could not see.

Level Up: Let the whispers speak clearly and reveal something unexpected.

---

5. The Day My Shadow Acted First

Visual description: A figure walking while the shadow takes a separate pose.

Story starter: His shadow reached out before he did, as if trying to warn him.

Level Up: Write what the shadow wants.

---

6. Sketches No One Knew I Drew

Visual description: A notebook filled with sketches of faces and scenes that feel too real.

Story starter: Someone had added a new sketch to her notebook. She had not drawn it.

Level Up: Describe the moment inside the mysterious sketch.

---

7. The Feeling I Could Not Explain

Visual description: A heart shape made of swirling mist that shifts unpredictably.

Story starter: A feeling wrapped itself around him, stronger than fear, softer than hope.

Level Up: Give the feeling a physical shape or voice.

---

8. The Locker That Opened on Its Own

Visual description: A locker door hangs slightly open, glowing faintly.

Story starter: The locker clicked open even though she had not touched it since yesterday.

Level Up: Reveal what the locker knows about the character.

---

9. A Secret I Almost Told

Visual description: A mouth partly covered by a hand with a soft glow behind the fingers.

Story starter: The secret sat at the edge of her voice, ready to spill out.

Level Up: Show what happens when she decides to reveal it or hold it in.

---

10. The Note Folded into a Strange Shape

Visual description: An origami star made from lined notebook paper.

Story starter: He found a folded note shaped like a star. Inside was one sentence written in his own handwriting.

Level Up: Write the message and explain how it appeared.

---

11. A Map of My Mood

Visual description: A shifting map with glowing paths that change color.

Story starter: Her mood changed and the map rearranged itself again.

Level Up: Describe a landmark in the character's emotional landscape.

---

12. The Dream That Would Not End

Visual description: A floating doorway surrounded by a soft dreamlike haze.

Story starter: He woke up, or at least he thought he did, until he saw the doorway from last night's dream.

Level Up: Let dream and reality collide.

13. Footsteps Behind Me That Were My Own

Visual description: A hallway with double sets of footprints following the same path.

Story starter: Someone followed her home. When she turned, no one was there, but the footsteps stayed.

Level Up: Reveal what the footsteps are trying to show her.

---

14. The Object I Should Have Thrown Away

Visual description: A tiny glowing trinket half hidden in a drawer.

Story starter: He kept it even though he knew he should not.

Level Up: Let the object change his emotions or actions.

---

15. The Double Life I Never Knew I Lived

Visual description: A split view of the same room in two different styles.

Story starter: She found a schedule written in her handwriting with events she did not remember attending.

Level Up: Write a scene from her other life.

16. The Song That Changed My Mind

Visual description: Headphones emit soft glowing sound waves.

Story starter: One song played that he had never heard before. The lyrics knew him too well.

Level Up: Write a few lines of the mysterious song.

---

17. A Lie That Became True

Visual description: A sticky note whose words slowly shift form.

Story starter: She told a harmless lie. The world adjusted to make it real.

Level Up: Show the moment the lie creates a new problem.

---

18. The Person Everyone Thinks I Am

Visual description: A silhouette filled with mismatched images that do not reflect the character.

Story starter: He read the comments about him and wondered who they were describing.

Level Up: Have him rewrite his own identity.

---

19. The Question I Could Not Answer

Visual description: A chalkboard with a single glowing question mark.

Story starter: When the question appeared, everyone knew who it was for.

Level Up: Let the answer surprise the character.

---

20. A Fear That Followed Me Home

Visual description: A faint shadow shape moving behind the character.

Story starter: The fear stayed with him long after the moment had passed.

Level Up: Give the fear a voice.

---

21. The Wish I Almost Whispered

Visual description: A candle flame leaning toward a character.

Story starter: She almost made a wish, and that was enough to begin something.

Level Up: Show what the half formed wish becomes.

---

22. The Symbol That Kept Appearing

Visual description: A geometric symbol chalked repeatedly on walls and sidewalks.

Story starter: He saw the symbol again. It was starting to feel personal.

Level Up: Reveal who draws it and why.

———————— • ♦ • ————————

23. A Message in My Handwriting I Did Not Write

Visual description: A notebook page shows writing identical to the character's.

Story starter: The message looked like her writing, except she had never written it.

Level Up: Write a response to the writer.

———————— • ♦ • ————————

24. A Room Where My Thoughts Echoed

Visual description: Translucent versions of the character's thoughts float through the room.

Story starter: Every thought came back to him in a soft echo.

Level Up: Choose one thought and let it take form.

———————— • ♦ • ————————

25. The Silence That Felt Too Loud

Visual description: A quiet scene with visible ripples in the air.

Story starter: The silence pressed against her like a heavy blanket.

Level Up: Let the silence hide a message.

26. A Promise I Made to Myself

Visual description: A glowing string tied around a wrist.

Story starter: He remembered the promise he once made as the string tightened.

Level Up: Show the cost of breaking the promise.

27. A Truth I Did Not See Coming

Visual description: A cracked mask rests on a table.

Story starter: She lifted the mask and realized it belonged to her.

Level Up: Reveal the truth the mask represents.

28. The Part of Me I Hid

Visual description: A locked box with faint light glowing under the lid.

Story starter: He hid the box because he knew what it contained.

Level Up: Describe the hidden part as if it were alive.

29. The Mirror That Showed Tomorrow

Visual description: A mirror shows a slightly changed version of the room.

Story starter: In the reflection, something had moved that had not moved in real life.

Level Up: Write the moment reality catches up.

30. The Moment I Became Brave

Visual description: A silhouette takes a steady step forward.

Story starter: She never thought she would find the courage, yet here she was.

Level Up: Show how bravery alters the moment.

Chapter 2
Friends and Drama

Friendships shape the way we see the world and the way we see ourselves. They can be supportive, complicated, unpredictable, and full of emotional turning points.

> This section explores connection, misunderstanding, loyalty, conflict, and the moments that reveal who people really are.

Each prompt places characters in social situations that spark questions and tension. Notice the emotions in the visual spark and let them guide your scene.

"The Group Chat Meltdown"

31. The Group Chat Meltdown

Visual description: A phone screen shows a fast scrolling group chat filled with overlapping messages, emojis, and alerts.

Story starter: By the time she opened the chat, the plan had already fallen apart.

Level Up: Write the scene using only dialogue from the chat.

---

32. A Promise Broken by Accident

Visual description: Two hands reaching toward each other across a desk, one pulling away slightly.

Story starter: They had promised to keep the secret. One slip changed everything.

Level Up: Show both sides of the story.

---

33. The Friend Who Stopped Talking

Visual description: Two lockers side by side, one decorated with photos, the other empty and closed.

Story starter: He walked past her without looking at her for the third day in a row.

Level Up: Reveal what made the silence begin.

34. A Conflict No One Wanted to Admit

Visual description: A crowded cafeteria table with two empty chairs pulled back from the group.

Story starter: Everyone felt the tension but pretended not to notice.

Level Up: Let a minor character trigger the truth.

---

35. A Secret Shared in Confidence

Visual description: Two friends sitting under a tree, one leaning in, the other looking unsure.

Story starter: She whispered the secret thinking it would stay safe. She was wrong.

Level Up: Reveal what the secret is and why it matters.

---

36. The Day Our Inside Joke Turned Outside

Visual description: A sheet of paper taped to a wall with a drawing that resembles the friends' inside joke.

Story starter: Their private joke appeared all over school. No one knew who put it there.

Level Up: Write the conversation when they discover it.

37. The Disappearing Partner in a Project

Visual description: A messy desk showing half completed project materials and one empty chair.

Story starter: He was supposed to help, but he had not shown up in a week.

Level Up: Reveal the reason for the disappearance.

38. A Misread Message at the Worst Time

Visual description: A phone with a notification bubble that cuts off mid sentence.

Story starter: She misunderstood the message and reacted before she could ask for clarity.

Level Up: Rewrite the story from the sender's perspective.

39. The Argument That Started Over Nothing

Visual description: Two mugs on a table, one turned over, tea spilled across the surface.

Story starter: The argument began with a single careless comment.

Level Up: Let the real reason for the argument surface later.

40. A Friendship Built on a Dare

Visual description: A scrap of notebook paper with the word "Dare" written boldly.

Story starter: Their friendship began the moment he accepted the dare.

Level Up: Explain why the dare changed everything.

---

41. The Person We Should Not Have Trusted

Visual description: A person standing slightly apart from a group, holding a folder behind their back.

Story starter: We trusted the wrong person and the truth came out fast.

Level Up: Show the moment trust breaks.

---

42. A Confession Sent to the Wrong Person

Visual description: A message with a heart icon next to a name that should not have been chosen.

Story starter: He hit send before he realized the name was not hers.

Level Up: Write both reactions.

43. The Afternoon Everything Shifted

Visual description: A park bench with backpacks tossed aside, one tipped over.

Story starter: Something small happened that changed the way they saw each other.

Level Up: Let the shift be subtle but meaningful.

---

44. A Hidden Talent Revealed

Visual description: A stage with a single spotlight and a figure standing uncertainly in the center.

Story starter: No one knew what she could do until that moment.

Level Up: Describe the reactions of at least three characters.

---

45. The Truth Behind an Unexpected Compliment

Visual description: Two speech bubbles overlapping. One bright, one slightly dimmed.

Story starter: The compliment sounded kind, but something about it felt off.

Level Up: Reveal the intention behind the words.

46. My Best Friend's Worst Idea

Visual description: A scribbled plan drawn on a whiteboard that looks chaotic and incomplete.

Story starter: He promised it would work. It did not.

Level Up: Show how the narrator tries to fix the consequences.

---

47. The Apology I Did Not Know How to Give

Visual description: An unsigned note with "I am sorry" written carefully in the center.

Story starter: She tried to write an apology but kept crossing out every version.

Level Up: Write the apology she finally sends.

---

48. A Reunion That Did Not Go as Planned

Visual description: Two friends running toward each other but one slows down suddenly.

Story starter: He thought they would pick up where they left off. They did not.

Level Up: Reveal what changed during their time apart.

49. Two Friends. Two Stories. One Event.

Visual description: A split illustration of the same moment seen from two angles.

Story starter: They remembered the day differently, and each believed their version was true.

Level Up: Write a short paragraph from each perspective.

50. The Mystery of the Missing Backpack

Visual description: An empty chair with a single strap of a backpack visible behind it.

Story starter: Her backpack was gone, but the strange part was what had been left in its place.

Level Up: Explain why the item was left.

51. The Pact We Swore to Keep

Visual description: Three hands stacked together in a promise gesture.

Story starter: We made a pact months ago. Now one of us had broken it.

Level Up: Reveal the pact in dialogue.

52. The Rumor That Spread Too Fast

Visual description: Speech bubbles branching out like a web.

Story starter: The rumor grew bigger every time someone repeated it.

Level Up: Write the moment someone confronts the source.

---

53. The Photo No One Wanted Posted

Visual description: A blurry photo on a phone screen with shocked emoji reactions.

Story starter: Someone posted the photo before anyone could stop them.

Level Up: Show the chain reaction it creates.

---

54. My Friend's Strange New Habit

Visual description: A friend hiding something behind their back while trying to act casual.

Story starter: She noticed the habit gradually. By then it was too late to ignore.

Level Up: Let the habit reveal a secret.

55. The Competition That Got Too Serious

Visual description: A scoreboard with two names tied for first place.

Story starter: It started as friendly fun. It did not end that way.

Level Up: Write the final round.

---

56. A Day Without My Phone

Visual description: A phone face down on a table with the battery icon glowing red.

Story starter: He lost the phone and discovered something about himself without it.

Level Up: Show how another person is affected too.

---

57. A Friend Who Needed Help but Would Not Ask

Visual description: A person sitting alone under a stairwell, head down.

Story starter: She knew something was wrong, but her friend insisted everything was fine.

Level Up: Let the truth appear through small clues.

---

58. The Party We Should Not Have Attended

Visual description: A doorway with bright lights inside and shadows of people moving.

Story starter: We knew we should not go, but we went anyway.

Level Up: Write the scene where everything turns.

---

59. The Unexpected Goodbye

Visual description: A bus pulling away while someone stands still on the sidewalk.

Story starter: She said goodbye so quickly that he did not have time to respond.

Level Up: Write the message he sends after she leaves.

---

60. A Moment That Saved a Friendship

Visual description: Two hands reaching toward each other, one uncertain, one steady.

Story starter: After everything that happened, one small choice pulled them back together.

Level Up: Show how both characters feel during the moment.

Chapter 3
Future Worlds

This section explores the worlds that might exist someday. Some are hopeful. Some are unsettling. Some feel like reflections of our own world taken a few steps forward.

> Technology, inventions, altered environments, advanced communication, and futuristic choices create stories filled with possibility and risk.

Let the visuals guide you into settings where ordinary characters face extraordinary realities. The future is not just about machines. It is about people living inside the unknown.

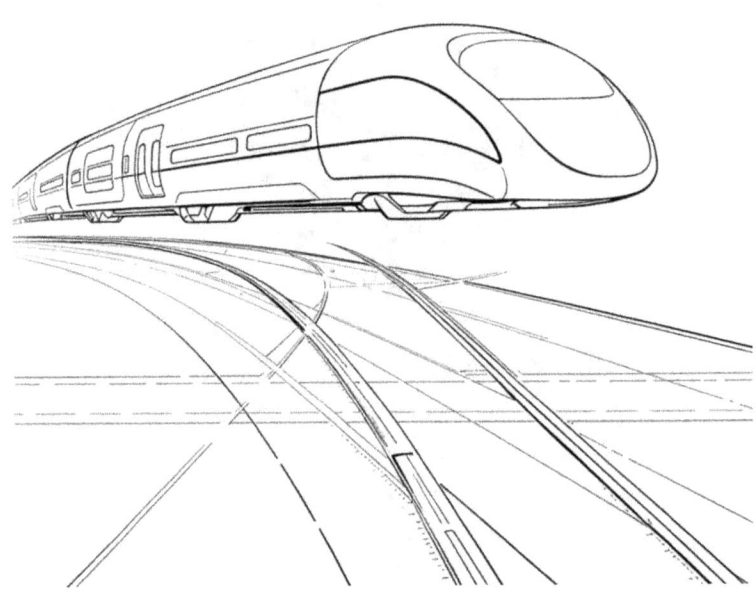

"The Train That Floated In Silence"

61. The Train That Floated In Silence

Visual description: A sleek floating train hovers above glowing tracks, completely soundless.

Story starter: The train arrived without a single sound, which meant something impossible was happening.

Level Up: Describe the first person who steps off the silent train.

---

62. A Message Sent Before It Was Invented

Visual description: A small device with a flashing message icon, connected to nothing.

Story starter: The message arrived on a device no one had ever seen before.

Level Up: Reveal who sent the message and from when.

---

63. The Day the Sky Changed Color

Visual description: A city skyline under a sky that shifts through unexpected colors.

Story starter: The sky turned a shade no one could name and the world paused to watch.

Level Up: Show how the color affects people or technology.

64. A Robot With an Impossible Request

Visual description: A humanoid robot kneels with glowing eyes, holding an object out to a human.

Story starter: The robot approached her quietly and asked for something robots were not supposed to want.

Level Up: Reveal why the robot has the request.

---

65. The Device That Predicted My Mood

Visual description: A wristband with shifting colored lights that react to emotion.

Story starter: The new device glowed bright red even though he felt calm.

Level Up: Show how someone else reacts to the reading.

---

66. A City That Never Sleeps and Never Stops

Visual description: Moving sidewalks, high speed lights, and tall neon buildings crowded together.

Story starter: The city kept moving day and night, and she was the only one who noticed something slowing down.

Level Up: Describe what happens when the slowdown spreads.

67. The Machine That Read My Memories

Visual description: A futuristic headset connected to a floating holographic screen displaying memories.

Story starter: He watched his own memories appear in front of him, one by one, even the ones he had forgotten.

Level Up: Let one memory appear that should not exist.

---

68. A Future Version of Me Arrives Too Soon

Visual description: Two versions of the same person face each other, one older and one younger.

Story starter: She stepped forward and faced someone she recognized instantly. Herself.

Level Up: Write the first words the future version says.

---

69. The App That Controlled Everything

Visual description: A phone screen with icons linked by glowing lines that spread across the image like a web.

Story starter: The newest app promised to make life easier. It did, until it made things too easy.

Level Up: Let the app make a decision without permission.

70. A Lab Accident No One Could Explain

Visual description: A cracked glass container filled with strange iridescent smoke.

Story starter: The accident left a mark on the room and on him too.

Level Up: Show how the accident changes one of his senses.

———————— • ♦ • ————————

71. The Last Tree in the World

Visual description: A single glowing tree inside a transparent dome in a barren landscape.

Story starter: People traveled from everywhere to see the last tree. She came to ask it a question.

Level Up: Have the tree respond in some way.

———————— • ♦ • ————————

72. A Hologram That Glitched to Life

Visual description: A hologram flickers, gaining unexpected color and depth.

Story starter: The hologram of a stranger glitched once, then breathed.

Level Up: Write how the stranger reacts to being seen.

———————— • ♦ • ————————

73. The Countdown That Started at Midnight

Visual description: A digital clock on a tower begins counting down from an unknown number.

Story starter: No one knew what the countdown was for, but everyone felt the urgency.

Level Up: Reveal who understands the countdown's meaning.

---

74. A Portal Hidden in Plain Sight

Visual description: A shimmering outline in the air behind a school fence.

Story starter: He noticed the shimmer only because he walked home a different way.

Level Up: Write what happens when he touches it.

---

75. The Drone That Followed Me Home

Visual description: A small drone hovers behind a character at a cautious distance.

Story starter: The drone followed her for three blocks before she finally turned around.

Level Up: Reveal what the drone is searching for.

76. A Mission to Fix Tomorrow

Visual description: A futuristic tablet displays a timeline with gaps and errors.

Story starter: He had one task: repair the future before the deadline.

Level Up: Describe the first mistake he must correct.

---

77. The Day School Was Replaced by Simulations

Visual description: Students sit in chairs wearing thin simulation glasses with virtual screens floating around them.

Story starter: School felt easier in the simulations until the system glitched and locked her inside the program.

Level Up: Write a scene where she tests the limits of the simulation.

---

78. An Upgrade I Did Not Ask For

Visual description: A wrist or eye interface shows a new feature labeled Upgrade Active.

Story starter: He woke up with a new ability that his device claimed was part of an automatic update.

Level Up: Show the first time the upgrade misfires.

79. The Future That Should Not Exist

Visual description: A city made of mismatched architectural styles, as if built from several timelines.

Story starter: She stood in a place where nothing matched what she remembered about the world.

Level Up: Reveal which timeline she belongs to.

---

80. A World Where Time Works Backward

Visual description: People walking backward in a street scene, clocks reversed, events unspooling.

Story starter: Time moved in reverse here, except for him.

Level Up: Write the moment someone notices he is moving forward.

---

81. The Note From an Unknown Planet

Visual description: A metallic envelope with symbols that glow faintly.

Story starter: The note fell from the sky during a quiet afternoon.

Level Up: Have the message reveal something personal.

---

82. A Neighborhood Where No One Ages

Visual description: A row of identical houses with families who appear the same in old and new photographs.

Story starter: No one in the neighborhood had aged in years, except her.

Level Up: Describe what she sees that others cannot.

---

83. The AI That Chose Me

Visual description: A glowing cube sits in front of the character, projecting a soft pulse of light.

Story starter: The AI selected him as its partner and no one knew why.

Level Up: Write the first instruction the AI gives.

---

84. The Memory They Tried to Delete

Visual description: A screen shows a memory file labeled Delete Failed.

Story starter: She was supposed to forget everything, but one memory stayed.

Level Up: Show how she hides the memory from others.

85. A Storm That Spoke in Numbers

Visual description: Lightning forms patterns that resemble coded messages.

Story starter: The storm came in with flashes that spelled out something only he could read.

Level Up: Translate part of the code.

---

86. The First Law I Refused to Obey

Visual description: A digital poster shows a list of laws with one glowing brightly.

Story starter: Everyone followed the laws without question, until she broke the one that mattered most.

Level Up: Reveal what the law protects.

---

87. A Glimpse of the World After Ours

Visual description: An image that shows a futuristic landscape growing over old ruins.

Story starter: He saw the future in a single blink, and it was nothing like he imagined.

Level Up: Write the moment he tries to return to the present.

88. The Experiment I Was Not Supposed to See

Visual description: A hidden lab with a chamber glowing a bright, unnatural light.

Story starter: She opened the wrong door and saw something still forming inside the chamber.

Level Up: Reveal who or what is inside.

---

89. The Hidden City Below Our Feet

Visual description: A secret underground city lit by neon signs and soft artificial skylight.

Story starter: He stepped through a maintenance hatch and found a whole world no one talked about.

Level Up: Describe the first person he meets below.

---

90. A Choice That Changed the Timeline

Visual description: A set of branching digital paths leading in different directions.

Story starter: The timeline shifted the moment she made her choice.

Level Up: Write what the original timeline would have been.

Chapter 4
What If

Morgan Hale

This section explores alternate realities, impossible moments, surreal twists, and questions that bend the rules of the world.

Every prompt begins with a small shift in reality and asks what might happen next.

These scenes invite wonder, curiosity, surprise, and creativity. Let the visuals push you into places where anything can happen and the ordinary is never what it seems. The stories in this section come from the question that starts every imaginative adventure: What if?

"What If?"

91. A Door That Opens Somewhere New Each Day

Visual description: A single wooden door standing alone in a forest clearing with a soft glow around the frame.

Story starter: Every day the door opened to a different place, and today he finally stepped through.

Level Up: Describe the place he discovers and how it reacts to him.

---

92. The World Where Everyone Knows Your Thoughts

Visual description: People walking with visible thought bubbles floating above their heads.

Story starter: She learned to control her thoughts carefully until the day one escaped on its own.

Level Up: Write the moment someone reacts to her thought.

---

93. A Day That Repeats for One Person Only

Visual description: A clock face showing the same time in multiple overlapping layers.

Story starter: He woke up to the same day again but everyone else kept moving forward.

Level Up: Describe what he does to break the cycle.

94. The Wish That Worked Too Well

Visual description: A single coin glows at the bottom of a wishing fountain.

Story starter: She wished for something simple, and then it came true in a way she never wanted.

Level Up: Show how she tries to undo the wish.

95. The Stranger Who Knows Your Name

Visual description: A mysterious figure standing on a street corner, holding a sign with a name written on it.

Story starter: The stranger called his name even though they had never met.

Level Up: Reveal the stranger's connection.

96. The Sky That Falls in Pieces

Visual description: Tilted fragments of sky reflecting different colors floating downward.

Story starter: Small pieces of the sky fell around her like broken glass.

Level Up: Write what happens when she touches one.

97. A Gift No One Wants

Visual description: A wrapped present sitting alone on a table, glowing faintly.

Story starter: The gift appeared every morning no matter where he hid it.

Level Up: Reveal what is inside the gift.

---

98. The Day Gravity Took a Break

Visual description: Everyday objects float gently around a living room.

Story starter: She woke up weightless and saw her belongings drifting above her.

Level Up: Show the world outside her home.

---

99. A Creature Only I Can See

Visual description: A small glowing creature sits beside the character, invisible to others.

Story starter: The creature followed him everywhere but refused to speak.

Level Up: Describe the creature's purpose.

100. The Moment the Moon Disappeared

Visual description: A night sky missing its moon with an empty circle where it once was.

Story starter: The moon vanished and the world held its breath.

Level Up: Write the first sign that something is wrong.

---

101. A Trail of Clues Left by Future Me

Visual description: A row of handwritten notes scattered along a sidewalk, each marked with a symbol.

Story starter: She found the first clue taped to her front door. It was in her own handwriting.

Level Up: Reveal what future her is trying to prevent.

---

102. A Clock That Runs on Secrets

Visual description: A clock with shifting symbols instead of numbers and a keyhole in the center.

Story starter: The clock would not tick until he whispered a secret into the keyhole.

Level Up: Write the secret he chooses.

103. The Island That Moves at Night

Visual description: A map with an island that appears in a different location every morning.

Story starter: She woke to find the island had drifted again and was now dangerously close.

Level Up: Describe who lives on the moving island.

---

104. The Doorbell That Rings by Itself

Visual description: A doorbell glowing a soft white light with no one outside.

Story starter: The bell rang every night at the same time even though no one was there.

Level Up: Reveal what happens when she finally opens the door in time.

---

105. A New Law of Nature Announced by Mistake

Visual description: A science classroom chalkboard shows a strange formula with a circle drawn around it.

Story starter: Someone wrote the formula as a joke but the world started following it.

Level Up: Show how the new law changes one important thing.

106. The World Built on Opposites

Visual description: Two halves of a city divided perfectly down the center, each side inverted in style.

Story starter: In this world everything had an opposite and everyone had one too.

Level Up: Write about the character's opposite.

---

107. A Book That Writes Back

Visual description: An open book with words appearing across the page on their own.

Story starter: He wrote a sentence and the book responded with one of its own.

Level Up: Write a short conversation between them.

---

108. The Painting That Changed Its Scene

Visual description: A framed painting with shifting landscapes inside.

Story starter: The painting changed again, this time showing a place she had visited yesterday.

Level Up: Reveal why the painting is tracking her.

---

109. My Life If One Choice Had Changed

Visual description: A mirror split into two versions of the same person.

Story starter: He saw what his life could have been if he had chosen differently.

Level Up: Write the moment he faces his alternate self.

---

110. A Stranger Who Knows My Past

Visual description: A figure reading from a notebook that has pages filled with dates and names.

Story starter: She introduced herself and listed memories he had never spoken aloud.

Level Up: Discover how she learned them.

---

111. A Street That Appears Only on Tuesdays

Visual description: A narrow cobblestone street with lanterns that glow only one day a week.

Story starter: The street appeared again, lined with shops that did not exist yesterday.

Level Up: Describe one shop in detail.

112. A Pet That Talks Only When Unseen

Visual description: A pet sitting in plain sight and a speech bubble floating behind it.

Story starter: The pet never spoke when someone was looking but its voice filled the empty room.

Level Up: Reveal what the pet wants to tell the character.

---

113. The Storm That Delivered a Message

Visual description: A lightning strike forms a clear shape or letter in the sky.

Story starter: The storm rolled in with a message she knew was meant for her.

Level Up: Write the meaning behind the storm's message.

---

114. A Place Where No One Can Lie

Visual description: A market filled with glowing symbols that dim whenever someone speaks.

Story starter: In this town every lie flickered into silence before it could be spoken.

Level Up: Show a character who tries to lie anyway.

115. The Memory I Borrowed

Visual description: A glass orb containing a swirling memory inside.

Story starter: He held the borrowed memory and felt someone else's emotions rush through him.

Level Up: Write the moment he realizes the memory belongs to someone he knows.

---

116. A World Without Noise

Visual description: A city where all movement is silent, with visible ripples in the air but no sound.

Story starter: She woke to a world without sound, as if someone had turned off the volume.

Level Up: Describe what happens when she tries to shout.

---

117. The Day Every Color Faded

Visual description: A town drained of color, shown in grayscale except for a single glowing object.

Story starter: The world turned colorless except for the item in his pocket.

Level Up: Reveal why this object keeps its color.

---

118. A Secret That Unlocks a New Reality

Visual description: A key that changes shape as it is rotated.

Story starter: She whispered a secret and the key shifted into a new form.

Level Up: Describe the reality it unlocks.

---

119. A Game That Controls Real Life

Visual description: A holographic game board overlays the real world with glowing tiles.

Story starter: Every move he made in the game changed something around him.

Level Up: Write the moment the game sets a challenge he cannot ignore.

---

120. The Visitor From Another Version of Me

Visual description: Two identical figures meet, one with slightly altered clothes or expression.

Story starter: She looked up and saw herself standing at the door, older and more confident.

Level Up: Write the warning the visitor brings.

Chapter 5
First Times

The first time we try something new, something shifts. First experiences can feel exciting, terrifying, awkward, or unforgettable.

They can change how we see ourselves or how we see the world.

This section is filled with moments of beginning. They might be small milestones or life changing steps. Use the visuals to sense the emotion behind the moment and follow the story into discovery.

"The First Moment I Realized I Was Wrong"

121. My First Day Somewhere Unexpected

Visual description: A student stands in front of a school or building they have never seen before, holding a schedule with unfamiliar room numbers.

Story starter: His first day was supposed to be ordinary, yet he had no idea where he had arrived.

Level Up: Write the moment he realizes this place is different from any school he has known.

122. The First Time I Broke a Rule

Visual description: A sign with rules posted clearly and one rule is subtly crossed out or smudged.

Story starter: She broke the rule on purpose, even though she had always followed them.

Level Up: Show the instant she decides she cannot go back.

123. The First Person I Ever Trusted

Visual description: Two characters sitting on a bench, one leaning forward as if sharing a vulnerable moment.

Story starter: He told her something he had never shared with anyone.

Level Up: Describe the moment she earns his trust.

124. The First Moment I Realized I Was Wrong

Visual description: A reflection in a window shows the character looking unsure.

Story starter: She believed she understood the story until one detail proved her wrong.

Level Up: Reveal the detail that changes everything.

---

125. My First Real Adventure

Visual description: A backpack sits beside open terrain with a marked trail stretching ahead.

Story starter: He started walking without knowing where the path would lead.

Level Up: Describe the first challenge he meets on the trail.

---

126. The First Time I Saved Someone

Visual description: A hand reaching out to grasp another hand on the edge of a drop or cliff.

Story starter: She did not think of herself as brave until the moment she reached out.

Level Up: Write the thoughts she has in the exact moment of grabbing the hand.

---

127. A First Impression That Was Not True

Visual description: Two characters meeting, one smiling awkwardly, the other looking uncertain.

Story starter: His first impression was completely wrong, and now he had to admit it.

Level Up: Reveal what the character misjudged.

---

128. The First Time I Faced a Fear

Visual description: A character standing at the top of a diving board, looking down at the water.

Story starter: She had avoided this moment for years. Now there was no turning back.

Level Up: Write how she feels the second she jumps.

---

129. My First Standing Ovation

Visual description: A stage with bright lights and dim silhouettes in the audience rising to their feet.

Story starter: The applause felt unreal, like it belonged to someone else.

Level Up: Write what she remembers most about the performance.

---

130. The First Message From Someone Unexpected

Visual description: A phone buzzes with a message from a name the character has not seen in a long time.

Story starter: The message was short, but it changed his entire evening.

Level Up: Reveal the full message.

---

131. The First Time I Got Lost on Purpose

Visual description: A map folded open with pencil markings added that do not match the printed lines.

Story starter: She stepped off the usual path just to see what would happen.

Level Up: Write what she discovers when she lets herself wander.

---

132. My First Big Mistake

Visual description: A broken object on the floor and hands covering a shocked face.

Story starter: He had no excuse. He had made a mistake that could not be undone.

Level Up: Describe the person who discovers the mistake.

133. The First Time I Tried Something New

Visual description: A character stands in front of shelves filled with unfamiliar items.

Story starter: She hesitated, tried it anyway, and everything shifted.

Level Up: Write about the moment she realizes she enjoys the new experience.

---

134. A First Kiss That Did Not Happen as Planned

Visual description: A bench in a quiet corner with a soft evening light falling through the trees.

Story starter: The moment came, then slipped away before either of them could reach for it.

Level Up: Write what stops the moment and how they react.

---

135. The First Time I Was Truly Honest

Visual description: A character stands in front of another, speaking with clear emotion.

Story starter: One truthful sentence felt harder than anything he had said before.

Level Up: Reveal the truth he chooses to say.

136. My First Mystery to Solve

Visual description: A clue sits on a desk: a key, a note, or a strange object.

Story starter: She did not mean to start an investigation, but the clue begged to be solved.

Level Up: Write the first step she takes in her investigation.

---

137. The First Time I Did Not Quit

Visual description: A track, trail, or obstacle course with a determined character pushing forward.

Story starter: He wanted to stop, but for once he kept going.

Level Up: Describe the moment he realizes he will finish.

---

138. A First Day That Felt Like a Movie

Visual description: A hallway with dramatic lighting, as if cinematic effects were added.

Story starter: Everything about the day felt larger than life.

Level Up: Describe one scene where reality feels unreal.

---

139. The First Time I Took the Blame

Visual description: A character stands in front of a group while everyone looks on, surprised.

Story starter: She decided to admit the truth even though it was not entirely her fault.

Level Up: Explain why she chooses to take the blame.

---

140. My First Real Discovery

Visual description: A dusty attic or an old storage room with a mysterious object partly uncovered.

Story starter: He lifted the cloth and found something he could not explain.

Level Up: Write the significance of this discovery.

---

141. The First Time I Saw Someone Differently

Visual description: A silhouette of a classmate or friend, shown with a subtle halo or glow to represent new perspective.

Story starter: After that moment, she realized she had misunderstood him all along.

Level Up: Reveal what she notices that changes her understanding.

142. The First Time I Felt at Home

Visual description: A cozy room with soft light and signs of welcome, such as open arms or a warm smile.

Story starter: It took only a second for him to feel something he had never felt before.

Level Up: Describe what makes the space feel safe.

---

143. A First Step Toward Something Bigger

Visual description: A pathway leading into a bright horizon, with the character standing at the start.

Story starter: She took one step and knew she had begun something important.

Level Up: Write the moment she almost turns back but decides not to.

---

144. The First Time I Asked for Help

Visual description: A hand reaching out toward another hand ready to assist.

Story starter: He finally said the words he had never wanted to say.

Level Up: Describe how the helper responds.

145. My First Big Choice

Visual description: A crossroads with two paths that look equally uncertain.

Story starter: She stood at the split path knowing she could choose only one.

Level Up: Write the consequences of the choice she makes.

---

146. The First Time I Stood Up to Someone

Visual description: A character faces another who is taller or more imposing, yet stands firm.

Story starter: His voice shook but he spoke anyway.

Level Up: Write the exact words he uses to stand up.

---

147. A First Page in a New Chapter

Visual description: A journal lies open with a blank first page and a pen resting on top.

Story starter: She opened the journal and knew her story was about to change.

Level Up: Write the first line she writes in the journal.

148. My First Leap Without Looking

Visual description: A character mid jump across a gap with a surprised expression.

Story starter: He leaped before he thought and hoped instinct would guide him.

Level Up: Write what he discovers on the other side.

---

149. A First Time That Changed Everything

Visual description: A moment frozen in time, such as a character stepping through a doorway or holding a symbolic object.

Story starter: She did not realize how important that first moment would become.

Level Up: Tell the future impact of that moment.

---

150. The First Promise I Meant to Keep

Visual description: Two hands linked in a simple promise gesture.

Story starter: He made the promise and felt the weight of it settle in his chest.

Level Up: Show the first action he takes to keep the promise.

Chapter 6
Villains and Secrets

This section explores mystery, tension, hidden motives, and the complicated line between good and bad. Villains are not always who we expect.

> Secrets have weight, and they change things once revealed.

These prompts place characters in moments where truths are uncovered and choices define who they become. The visuals use shadow, contrast, and symbolic detail to build atmosphere. Let your scenes follow the suspense wherever it leads.

"A Secret Hidden in Plain Sight"

151. The Villain Who Saved the Day

Visual description: A dark silhouette reaches to pull someone to safety while crowds watch from the background.

Story starter: Everyone feared the villain, so no one understood why they had just saved her life.

Level Up: Write the reason the villain chose to help.

---

152. A Secret Hidden in Plain Sight

Visual description: A school hallway scene with a small symbol carved into a locker, unnoticed by most.

Story starter: The secret was right in front of him, but he only noticed it today.

Level Up: Reveal what the symbol means.

---

153. The Enemy Who Wanted My Help

Visual description: Two characters face each other across a table, one tense, one pleading.

Story starter: She was the last person he expected to ask for help, yet here she was.

Level Up: Write the request the enemy makes.

154. A Code Only One Person Can Break

Visual description: A coded message with symbols arranged in a pattern only the main character recognizes.

Story starter: The message was meaningless to everyone else but not to her.

Level Up: Reveal how she learned the code.

155. The Villain's Unexpected Weakness

Visual description: A shadowy figure flinches from a small object like a locket or charm.

Story starter: He discovered the villain had a weakness no one could have predicted.

Level Up: Show how he uses this knowledge.

156. A Hidden Room Under the School

Visual description: A trapdoor slightly open beneath a rug, glowing faintly from below.

Story starter: She stepped through the trapdoor and found a room that should not exist.

Level Up: Describe who built the room and why.

157. The Package I Was Told Not to Open

Visual description: A small sealed box with warning labels and a mysterious lock.

Story starter: He opened the package even though the instructions clearly said not to.

Level Up: Reveal what is inside and why it is dangerous.

———•♦•———

158. A Whisper in a Locked Hallway

Visual description: A dark school hallway with a single light flickering and soft whisper shapes curling through the air.

Story starter: The hallway was locked, yet someone whispered her name from inside.

Level Up: Write the whisper's message.

———•♦•———

159. The Rival Who Knows Too Much

Visual description: A rival character stands confidently, holding a closed notebook filled with secrets.

Story starter: His rival smiled because she knew something he did not want anyone to know.

Level Up: Reveal the secret the rival knows.

———•♦•———

160. The Secret Society With My Name on the List

Visual description: A parchment list pinned to a wall with glowing names, including the character's.

Story starter: Her name appeared on the list even though she never joined.

Level Up: Describe the initiation she faces.

---

161. A Confession Found in Ashes

Visual description: A half burned letter on a desk, edges still smoking lightly.

Story starter: The confession survived just enough for him to read the first line.

Level Up: Write the rest of the confession.

---

162. A Plan That Went Too Far

Visual description: A whiteboard filled with diagrams and arrows, some crossed out, some circled urgently.

Story starter: Their plan started small, but now it had grown into something dangerous.

Level Up: Show the moment the plan crosses the line.

163. The Disappearance No One Mentions

Visual description: A school desk sits empty with a single item left behind, like a bracelet or pencil.

Story starter: Someone had vanished and everyone acted like they never existed.

Level Up: Write about the one person who remembers them.

164. The Enemy With a Familiar Face

Visual description: A shadowed figure reveals a face that looks just like the main character.

Story starter: She froze when she realized her enemy looked exactly like her.

Level Up: Write the first exchange of words between them.

165. The Truth Buried in the Attic

Visual description: An old attic with dust, cobwebs, and a trunk slightly open.

Story starter: He had avoided the attic for years, but today the truth waited for him there.

Level Up: Reveal what he finds inside the trunk.

166. A Deal With Someone Dangerous

Visual description: Two hands shake in a dark alley, one hand noticeably gloved or marked.

Story starter: She made a deal she knew she should not have made.

Level Up: Describe the exact terms of the deal.

---

167. The Villain's Last Warning

Visual description: A torn note left behind with jagged handwriting.

Story starter: The villain left a warning that felt more like a promise.

Level Up: Write how the main character responds to the warning.

---

168. A Mystery Carved in Stone

Visual description: A stone wall etched with unfamiliar symbols that glow when touched.

Story starter: The carvings lit up under his hand, forming a message only he could read.

Level Up: Translate the full message.

---

169. The File I Should Not Have Read

Visual description: A computer screen displays a confidential file with a hidden folder open.

Story starter: She clicked the wrong folder and uncovered something that changed everything.

Level Up: Reveal the first line of the file.

---

170. Shadows That Move Without People

Visual description: Several shadows stretch across the floor even though no one stands near them.

Story starter: The shadows shifted on their own and crept toward him.

Level Up: Describe what the shadows want.

---

171. A Secret Meeting at Midnight

Visual description: A rooftop under the moonlight where two figures stand in hushed conversation.

Story starter: She arrived early and overheard something she should not have heard.

Level Up: Reveal what the meeting is about.

172. The Diary Left Behind by a Stranger

Visual description: A diary rests on a park bench with a name written inside that the character does not recognize.

Story starter: He opened the diary and read the first page. The diary knew his name.

Level Up: Write the next page of the diary.

---

173. A Clue Hidden in a Photograph

Visual description: A photograph of a group of people with one odd detail circled in red.

Story starter: She noticed something in the photo that everyone else had missed.

Level Up: Write the significance of the circled detail.

---

174. The Villain Who Wanted Forgiveness

Visual description: A cloaked figure kneels on the ground, placing their weapon aside.

Story starter: He did not expect the villain to ask for forgiveness.

Level Up: Write the reason the villain wants redemption.

175. A Code Word That Changes Everything

Visual description: A scrap of paper with a single word written boldly in the center.

Story starter: The code word slipped out by accident and everything shifted.

Level Up: Describe how the world or scene reacts to the code word.

———— • ♦ • ————

176. The Locked Box Under My Bed

Visual description: A wooden box with ornate metalwork and a heavy lock.

Story starter: She finally dared to look under her bed and found the box waiting for her.

Level Up: Write the moment she opens it.

———— • ♦ • ————

177. A Betrayal I Did Not See

Visual description: Two friends stand apart, one holding something they should not have.

Story starter: He trusted her completely. That is what made the betrayal hurt most.

Level Up: Reveal the motive behind the betrayal.

———— • ♦ • ————

178. The Secret That Protects Us

Visual description: A glowing symbol held between two hands, shining brightly.

Story starter: The secret kept everyone safe, but now it was starting to fade.

Level Up: Write how the characters try to protect the secret.

---

179. The Villain's Final Choice

Visual description: A crossroads at night with the villain standing alone, deciding between two paths.

Story starter: No one could predict what they would choose in their final moment.

Level Up: Write the choice and the result.

---

180. The Truth That Remains

Visual description: A cracked mask on the ground beside a photograph half hidden in shadows.

Story starter: When all the secrets fell away, one truth stayed behind.

Level Up: Reveal the truth and how it changes the character.

About the Author

Morgan Hale writes stories and creative resources for young people who want to explore imagination, identity, and possibility. With a background in education and youth creative development, the author believes that every teen has a voice worth hearing and a story worth telling. Their books are designed to help writers discover confidence, curiosity, and the joy of creative play.

When not writing, Morgan works with schools, libraries, and community programs to support young storytellers. They love notebooks, unexpected ideas, and conversations that turn into stories.

NOTES FOR EDUCATORS

This book supports writing practice in flexible and accessible ways. Educators may find these strategies helpful when integrating prompts into lessons:

Routine building

Ten minutes of daily writing builds stamina, fluency, and confidence. Students learn to begin writing without fear of the blank page.

Theme exploration

The six sections correspond loosely to identity development, social dynamics, speculative thinking, imagination, personal growth, and narrative tension. You can align them with curriculum topics or emotional learning themes.

Creative choice

Allowing students to choose their prompt increases engagement. Some will gravitate toward emotional scenes, others toward humor or suspense.

NOTES FOR EDUCATORS

Discussion and reflection

Before writing, display the visual spark and invite students to share what they notice. After writing, choose volunteers to read one sentence they feel proud of.

Revision

Once a week, have students selecting a previous entry to revise or expand. This fosters the writing process without overwhelming pressure.

Assessment

Daily entries should not be graded for correctness. Instead, consider participation based scoring or short positive comments that reinforce creativity and effort.

INDEX BY THEME

This index helps to locate prompts by the type of story you want to explore. Prompts may appear in multiple categories.

Identity and Emotion

1, 2, 3, 4, 7, 9, 11, 14, 15, 17, 18, 19, 20, 21, 22, 24, 26, 27, 28, 29, 30

Friendship and Relationships

31, 32, 33, 35, 36, 37, 38, 39, 42, 43, 44, 45, 47, 48, 49, 50, 51, 52, 53, 54, 56, 57, 59, 60

Mystery and Secrets

2, 10, 13, 22, 24, 35, 36, 49, 50, 71, 81, 84, 88, 95, 101, 103, 108, 110, 114, 115, 118, 122, 136, 140, 150, 155, 156, 157, 158, 163, 165, 169, 170, 171, 172, 173, 176, 178, 180

Adventure and Exploration

5, 12, 25, 41, 55, 61, 63, 68, 72, 74, 75, 76, 77, 85, 86, 87, 89, 90, 98, 103, 107, 121, 125, 131, 137, 138, 143, 148

INDEX BY THEME

Speculative and Science Fiction

63, 64, 66, 67, 69, 70, 71, 72, 73, 74, 77, 78, 79, 80, 81, 82, 83, 84, 85, 87, 89, 90

Fantasy and Magical Themes

3, 4, 11, 12, 14, 21, 24, 25, 28, 40, 70, 71, 72, 73, 74, 80, 88, 95, 96, 97, 99, 100, 102, 103, 104, 105, 106, 107, 108, 112, 113, 115, 116, 117, 118

Growing Up and First Experiences

121 through 150

Villains, Conflict, and Dramatic Tension

151 through 180 and also 46, 47, 55, 57

www.ingramcontent.com/pod-product-compliance
Lightning Source LLC
Chambersburg PA
CBHW051420070526
44584CB00023B/3514